DUMB
JOKES
for smart kids

MEGA
DUMB
JOKES
for smart kids

Buster Books

Compiled and edited by Philippa Wingate
Designed by Zoe Quayle
Cover illustration by Martin Chatterton

First published in Great Britain
in 2001 by Buster Books, an imprint
of Michael O'Mara Books Limited,
9 Lion Yard, Tremadoc Road,
London SW4 7NQ

A CIP catalogue record for this book is
available from the British Library.

ISBN 1–903840–31–7

1 3 5 7 9 10 8 6 4 2

Visit our website at
www.mombooks.com

Printed and bound by Bookmarque Ltd, UK

CONTENTS

What's black and white and red all over?

A sunburnt zebra.

Where do hamsters come from?

Hampsterdam.

What is the fastest thing in water?

A motor pike.

What do you get if you cross a spider with a computer?

A web page.

What's a puppy's favourite kind of pizza?

Pupperoni.

Which day do chickens hate most?

Fry-day.

Why do gorillas have big nostrils?

Because they have big fingers.

Why did the rooster cross the road?

Because it thought it was a chicken.

MOOOOO!

One evening a mother was reading a book about animals to her three-year-old son.

The mother said, "What does the cow say, Billy?"

Billy answered, "Moo!"

The mother then said, "Great! What does the cat say?"

Billy replied, "Meow."

The mother exclaimed, "Oh Billy, you're so smart! What does the frog say?"

The little three-year-old looked up at his mother with wide eyes and in his deepest voice replied, "Bud."

LOBSTER STORY

One day a fisherman is walking from the pier carrying two lobsters in a bucket. A game warden approaches him and asks to see his fishing licence. "I didn't catch these lobsters, they are my pets," says the fisherman. "Every day I come down to the water and whistle. These lobsters jump out and I take them for a walk."

The warden doesn't believe the fisherman and reminds him that it is illegal to fish without a licence.

The fisherman replies, "If you don't believe me then watch," and he throws the lobsters back into the water.

The warden says, "Now whistle to your lobsters and show me that they will come out of the water."

The fisherman turns to the warden and asks, "What lobsters?"

MOUSE MATTERS

A group of young children were sitting in a circle with their teacher. She was going around the class asking each of them a question.

First she asked, "Davy, what noise does a cow make?"
He responded, "It goes moo."

Then she asked, "Alice, what noise does a cat make?"
Alice replied, "It goes meow."

Next she asked, "Jamie, what sound does a lamb make?"
His response was, "It goes baa."

Finally she questioned one last child, "And Jennifer, what sound does a mouse make?"
Jennifer replied, "Er, it goes... click!"

Why did the chicken
cross the playground?

To get to the other slide.

Why does a flamingo
lift up one leg?

Because if it lifted
up both legs it would
fall over.

Why do birds fly
south in the winter?

Because it's too far
to walk.

What is a polygon?

A dead parrot.

What kind of snack do little monkeys have with their milk?

Chocolate chimp cookies.

What do you get when you cross a pig and a centipede?

Bacon and legs.

What's a cat's favourite breakfast?

Mice Krispies.

What do whales like to chew?

Blubber gum.

What do frogs eat with their hamburgers?

French flies.

What do cats like on their hot dogs?

Mouse-tard.

What is a little dog's favourite drink?

Pupsi-cola.

Why did Tigger jump down the toilet?

He was looking for Pooh.

What goes "Oooo, oooo, oooo?"

A cow with no lips.

What do you call a three-legged donkey?

A wonkey.

What is black and white, black and white, black and white?

A zebra caught in a revolving door.

What do dogs eat at the cinema?

Pup-corn.

I KNOW WHO YOU ARE!

A blind rabbit and a blind snake meet each other on the road one day.

The blind snake reaches out and touches the rabbit. He says, "Ah ha, you're soft and fuzzy and have floppy ears. You must be a rabbit."

The blind rabbit reaches out and touches the snake and says, "Ah ha, you're slimy, beady-eyed and low to the ground. You must be a maths teacher."

HOW HIGH?

A kangaroo named Skippy kept escaping from his enclosure at the zoo. Knowing that he could hop really high, the zoo officials built a two-metre fence. However, Skippy was out of his enclosure the next morning, roaming around the zoo.

A ten metre fence was put up. But again Skippy got out.

When the fence was thirty metres high, a camel in the next enclosure asked Skippy the kangaroo, "How much higher do you think they'll build it?"

Skippy replied, "They could build it 1000 metres high, but unless somebody locks the gate at night, I am going to keep getting out of my enclosure."

Why is the snail the strongest animal?

Because he carries a house on his back.

What did the slug say as he slipped down the wall?

How slime flies!

How do you know your kitchen floor is dirty?

Slugs leave a trail on the floor that reads "Clean me!"

18

What is the definition of a slug?

A snail with a housing problem!

What's the difference between school dinners and a pile of slugs?

School dinners come on a plate.

What do you do when two snails have a fight?

Leave them to slug it out.

What is the difference
between an elephant
and a flea?

An elephant can have
fleas, but a flea can't
have elephants.

What do you call a
friend with an elephant
on his head?

A flatmate.

How do you know
when there's an
elephant under your bed?

Your nose touches
the ceiling.

What do you call an elephant that flies?

A jumbo jet.

What do you get if you cross an elephant and a kangaroo?

Big holes all over Australia.

How does an elephant get down from a tree?

He sits on a leaf and waits until autumn.

Why did the elephant paint himself with lots of different colours?

Because he wanted to hide in the colouring box.

21

Why were the elephants thrown out of the swimming pool?

Because they couldn't hold their trunks up.

What time is it when an elephant sits on the fence?

Time to fix the fence.

Why does an elephant wear sneakers?

So that he can sneak up on mice.

DOCTOR, DOCTOR...

Doctor, Doctor, I swallowed
a bone.
    Are you choking?
No, I really did!

Doctor, Doctor, I've got wind!
Can you give me something?
    Yes – here's a kite.

Doctor, Doctor, how do I stop
my nose from running?
    Stick your foot out
    and trip it up!

Doctor, Doctor, I keep
getting pains in my eye
when I drink coffee.
    Have you tried taking
    the spoon out of your cup?

Doctor, Doctor, during the week I feel like a teepee and then at the weekend I feel like a wigwam.

You're too tents.

Doctor, Doctor, my little boy has just swallowed a roll of film from his camera.

Hmmmm. Let's hope that nothing develops.

Doctor, Doctor, my son has swallowed my ballpoint pen. What should I do?

Use a pencil until I get there.

Doctor, Doctor, when I press with my finger here... it hurts, and here... it hurts, and here... and here... What do you think is wrong with me?
    You have a broken finger.

Doctor, Doctor, I feel like a pair of curtains.
    Well, pull yourself together then.

Doctor, Doctor, I keep thinking I'm a dog.
    Sit on the couch and we will talk about it.
But I'm not allowed up on the couch.

Doctor, Doctor, I can't pronounce my F's, T's and H's.

Well, you can't say fairer than that then.

Doctor, Doctor, I've lost my memory.

When did this happen?

When did what happen?

Doctor, Doctor, I keep seeing double.

Please sit on the couch.

Which one?

Doctor, Doctor, I think I'm a telephone.

Well, take these pills and if they don't work, give me a ring!

Doctor, Doctor, I'm so ugly.
What can I do about it?
    Hire yourself out for
    Halloween parties!

Doctor, Doctor, I think I'm
a bridge.
    What has come over you?
Oh, two cars, a large truck and
a coach.

Doctor, Doctor, my wife thinks
she's a duck.
    You'd better bring her in to
    see me straight away.
I can't do that – she's already
flown south for the winter.

Doctor, Doctor, there's an
invisible ghost in the waiting
room.
    Tell him I can't see him
    without an appointment.

GHOULISH
GIGGLES

Why are ghosts afraid?

Because they have no guts.

How do you make a milk shake?

Sneak up behind it and say "Boo!"

What did the skeleton say to her boyfriend?

I love every bone in your body.

What happened at the vampire Olympics?

All the races finished neck and neck.

Which instrument does a skeleton play?

Trombone.

Who does a vampire fall in love with?

The girl necks door.

Why did Frankenstein squash his girlfriend?

He had a crush on her.

Which happened to the mad vampire?

He went a little batty.

What's a vampire's favourite sport?

Batminton.

Why didn't the skeleton go to the party?

He had no body to go with.

What is evil and ugly and bounces?

A witch on a trampoline.

What is evil and ugly on the inside and green on the outside?

A witch dressed as a cucumber.

What was written on the hypochondriac's tombstone?

"I told you I was ill!"

What do you call a ghost mother and father?

Transparents.

When can't you bury people who live opposite a graveyard?

When they're not dead.

What is a demon's favourite TV sitcom?

Fiends.

Why are graveyards so noisy?

Because of all the coffin.

Where do ghosts get an education?

High sghoul.

What do you call a skeleton who won't get up in the mornings?

Lazy bones.

What is the best way to get rid of a demon?

Exorcise a lot.

Which vampire ate the three bears' porridge?

Ghouldilocks.

What sort of bands do vampires join?

Blood groups.

What roads do ghosts live on?

Dead ends.

What flavour ice cream do vampires like?

Veinilla.

What did the ghost say to her son?

"Don't spook until you are spooken to."

What do you call a wizard from outer space?

A flying sorcerer.

How can you help a starving cannibal?

Give him a hand.

Why did the wizard wear red, white and blue braces?

To keep his trousers up.

What was the cannibal called who ate his father's sister?

An aunt-eater.

What did the cannibal mum say to her son who was chasing a missionary?

"Stop playing with your food."

DINOSAUR
JOKES

What do you get when dinosaurs crash their cars?

Tyrannosaurus wrecks.

What vehicle does T-Rex use to go from planet to planet?

A Dinosaucer.

What kind of materials do dinosaurs use for the floor of their homes?

Rep Tiles.

How do you ask a dinosaur to lunch?

Tea Rex?

What should you do if you find a dinosaur in your bed?

Sleep somewhere else.

What do you call a dinosaur who's been left in the rain?

A Stegosaurust.

How did the dinosaur feel after he ate a pillow?

Down in the mouth.

What are prehistoric monsters called when they sleep?

Dinosnores!

What did the dinosaur say when he saw the volcano explode?

"What a lavaly day."

What do you say to a twenty-ton dinosaur with headphones on?

Anything you want. He can't hear you.

Why did the dinosaur cross the road?

Because the chicken wasn't invented yet.

Do you know how long dinosaurs walked the planet?

Exactly the same as short dinosaurs.

What do you call a dinosaur with no eyes?

A doyouthinkhesaurus.

Why did dinosaurs eat raw meat?

Because they didn't know how to cook.

What does a
Triceratops sit on?

Its Tricer-bottom.

What do you get
if you cross a
dinosaur with a pig?

Jurassic Pork.

What do you get if a
dinosaur sneezes?

Out of the way.

What is as big as a
dinosaur, but
weighs nothing?

Its shadow.

What followed
the dinosaurs?

Their tails.

What do you get
when you cross a
dinosaur with
a bomb?

Dinomite.

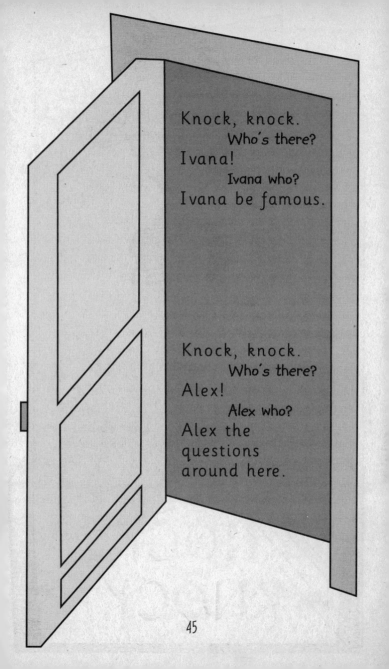

Knock, knock.
          Who's there?
Ivana!
          Ivana who?
Ivana be famous.

Knock, knock.
          Who's there?
Alex!
          Alex who?
Alex the
questions
around here.

45

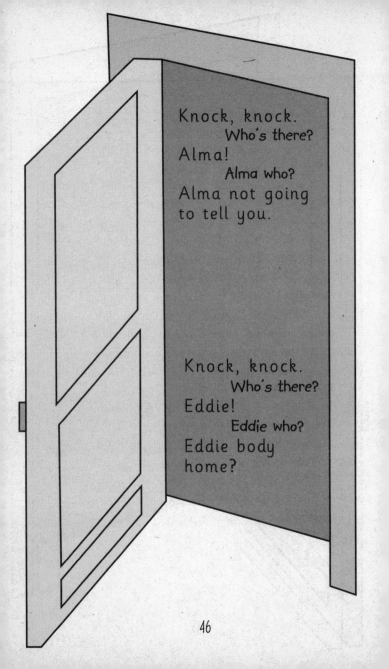

Knock, knock.
      Who's there?
Alma!
      Alma who?
Alma not going
to tell you.

Knock, knock.
      Who's there?
Eddie!
      Eddie who?
Eddie body
home?

Knock, knock.
    Who's there?
Harry!
    Harry who?
Harry up and
answer this door!

Knock, knock.
    Who's there?
Bertha!
    Bertha who?
Bertha-day
greetings!

48

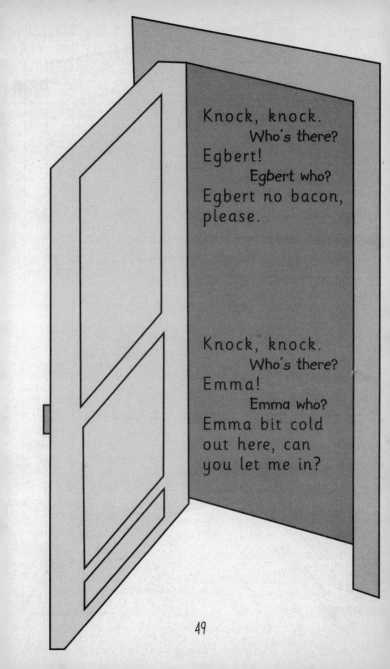

Knock, knock.
        Who's there?
Egbert!
        Egbert who?
Egbert no bacon,
please.

Knock, knock.
        Who's there?
Emma!
        Emma who?
Emma bit cold
out here, can
you let me in?

49

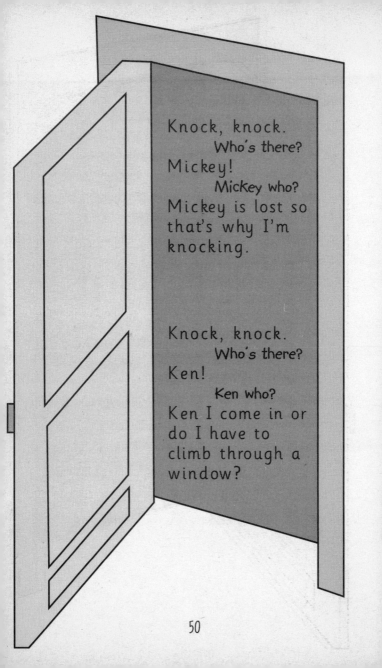

Knock, knock.
    Who's there?
Mickey!
    Mickey who?
Mickey is lost so
that's why I'm
knocking.

Knock, knock.
    Who's there?
Ken!
    Ken who?
Ken I come in or
do I have to
climb through a
window?

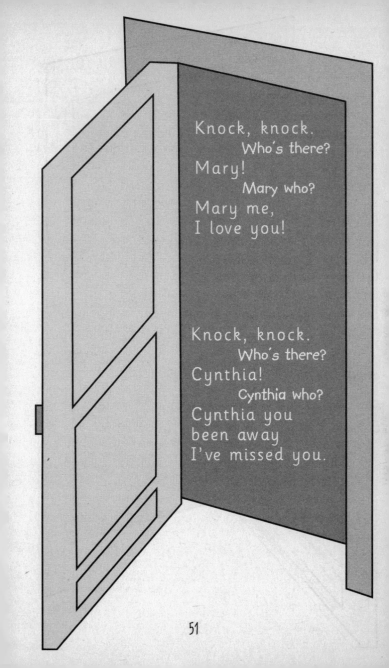

Knock, knock.
        Who's there?
Mary!
        Mary who?
Mary me,
I love you!

Knock, knock.
        Who's there?
Cynthia!
        Cynthia who?
Cynthia you
been away
I've missed you.

51

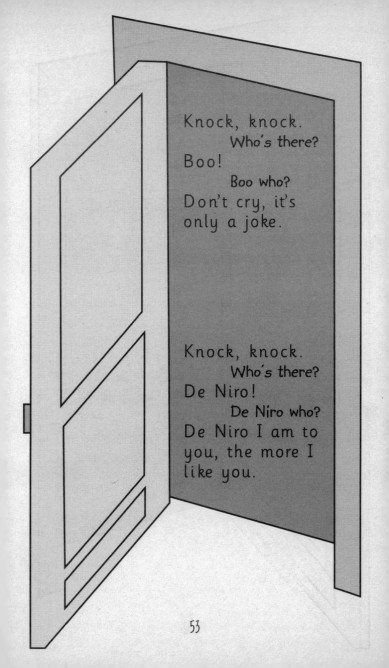

Knock, knock.
          Who's there?
Boo!
          Boo who?
Don't cry, it's
only a joke.

Knock, knock.
          Who's there?
De Niro!
          De Niro who?
De Niro I am to
you, the more I
like you.

53

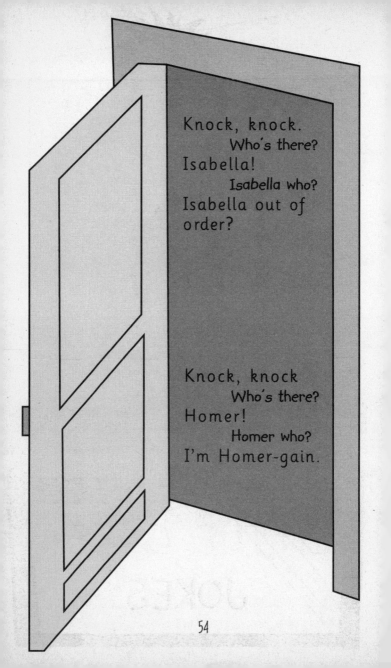

LITTLE GREEN JOKES

PARTY ON

Cool Teenage Martian: I was at a party on Mercury last night.

His Friend: Was it any good?

Cool Teenage Martian: No, it was really boring.

His Friend: How come?

Cool Teenage Martian: There was no atmosphere.

CLOSE ENCOUNTER

A woman was filling her car with petrol at a petrol station when she noticed a spaceship landing in front of her.

An alien stepped out of the spaceship and started to fill the craft with petrol.

The woman noticed the letters "U.F.O." printed on the side of the ship.

She turned to the alien and asked, "Does U.F.O. stand for Unidentified Flying Object?"

The alien answered, "No, it stands for Unleaded Fuel Only!"

What is an astronaut's favourite meal?
Launch.

Why couldn't the astronaut land on the moon?
It was already full.

What's the best way to speak to a Martian?
Long distance.

What's a Martian's normal eyesight?
20-20-20-20-20.

What kind of ticks do you find on the moon?
Luna-ticks.

BLAST OFF!

Three men were in a conference room at the NASA headquarters trying to decide the best way to spend £10 billion on space exploration.

"I think we should put our men on Mars," said the first man.

"Oh, good idea!" said the other two.

"I think we should put our men on Venus," said the second man.

"Oh, good idea!" said the other two.

"I think we should put our men on the Sun," said the third man.

"How will you do that? Won't they burn up?" asked the other two.

"No. We will go at night."

What's the best way to get straight A's?

Use a ruler.

How did the Vikings send secret messages?

By Norse code!

Pupil: My teacher was mad with me because I didn't know where the Rockies were.

Mother: Well, next time remember where you put things!

What would you get if you crossed a vampire and a teacher?

Lots of blood tests.

Dad: Why aren't you doing very well in history?

Kid: Because the teacher keeps asking about things that happened before I was born.

What's black and white all over and difficult?

An exam paper.

Who invented fractions?

Henry the 1/8th.

Teacher: What are the Great Plains?

Pupil: 747, Concorde and F-16.

What kind of lighting did Noah use for the ark?

Floodlights.

Teacher: Class, we will have only half a day of school this morning.

Class: Hooray.

Teacher: We will have the other half this afternoon!

Teacher: You aren't paying attention to me. Are you having trouble hearing?

Pupil: No, teacher. I am having trouble listening.

Son: I can't go to school today.

Father: Why not?

Son: I don't feel well.

Father: Where don't you feel well?

Son: In school.

Teacher: Are you good at multiplication?

Pupil: Yes and no.

Teacher: What do you mean?

Pupil: Yes, I'm no good at multiplication.

Why did Henry VIII have so many wives?

He liked to chop and change.

Teacher: Why is the Mississippi such an unusual river?

Pupil: Because it has four eyes and can't see.

Pupil (on the phone): My son has a bad cold and won't be able to come to school today.

School Secretary: Who is this speaking?

Pupil: This is my father speaking.

What did the Sheriff of Nottingham say when Robin fired at him?

That was an arrow escape.

What did Noah do while spending time on the ark?

Fished, but he didn't catch much. He only had two worms.

1st Roman Soldier: What is the time?

2nd Roman Soldier: XX past VII.

Teacher: You missed school yesterday, didn't you?

Pupil: Not very much.

Teacher: Where is your homework?

Pupil: I left it in my shirt and my mother put it in the washing machine.

Teacher: Where is your homework?

Pupil: Some aliens from outer space borrowed it so they could study how the human brain worked.

Teacher: Where is your homework?

Pupil: Our furnace stopped working and we had to burn it to stop ourselves from freezing.

Pupil: I can't solve this problem.

Teacher: Any five-year-old could solve this one.

Pupil: No wonder I can't do it then, I'm nearly ten.

Teacher: Did your parents help you with these homework problems?

Pupil: No, I got them all wrong by myself.

Father: How were the exam questions?

Son: Easy.

Father: Then why look so unhappy?

Son: The questions didn't give me any trouble, just the answers.

Did you hear about the teacher who had crossed eyes?

She couldn't control her pupils.

Why does my teacher wear sunglasses?

Because I am so bright.

Why did the teacher get an electric shock?

She stepped on a bun and a currant went up her leg.

Laugh and the class laughs with you. But you get to do detention alone.

What came after the Stone Age?

The sausage.

What's the longest sentence?

Life imprisonment.

What's the longest word?

Smiles - because there's a mile between the first and last letter.

Teacher: Jim, be sure that you go straight home.

Jim: I can't. I live around the corner.

What is the difference between frogspawn and school gravy?

Not a lot.

Teacher: Where is your homework?

Pupil: I lost it fighting this kid who said you weren't the best teacher in the school.

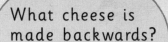

What cheese is made backwards?

Edam?

What is the best hand to write with?

Neither – it's best to write with a pen!

Did you hear about the fool who keeps going around saying "No"?
No.
Oh, so it's you!

Where does a general keep his armies?

Up his sleevies.

What is green, has four legs and two trunks?

Two seasick tourists.

What did the tie say to the hat?

You go on ahead and I'll hang around.

What's red and flies and wobbles at the same time?

A jelly copter.

What's the name for a short-legged tramp?

A low down bum.

How many rotten eggs does it take to make a stink bomb?

A phew!

Waiter, this soup tastes funny?

Then why aren't you laughing?

I want a hair cut please.

Certainly. Which one?

Why was the Egyptian girl worried?

Because her daddy was a mummy.

What has a bottom at the top?

I don't know?

Your legs.

Waiter, waiter, do you serve snails?

Sit down, sir, we serve anyone.

What cake wanted to rule the world?

Attila the Bun.

What do you call a man with a tree on his head?

Edwood.

OFF THE WALL

On a wall in a school yard
someone had scrawled —
Is there intelligent life on Earth?

A week later, someone else
added — Yes, but we are only
stopping to refuel.

SNAKE BITE

Boy: I once met a lion who had
been bitten by a snake.

Girl: What did he say?

Boy: Nothing, silly, lions don't
talk!

STRING-A-LING

Two pieces of string meet one day in the park. One plays on the slide, while the other plays on the swings.

They're having a great time, until one piece of string decides to go on the roundabout.

After a while, the string begins to feel really dizzy and falls off the roundabout, scraping across the tarmac and making a tangled mess of one of its ends. Finally it falls in a heap on the ground.

The second piece of string looks at him and sighs, "You're not very good on that roundabout are you?"

The first string looks at himself and says, "I'm a frayed knot."

What lies at the bottom of the sea and whimpers?

A nervous wreck.

What do you call a woman who steals cows?

A beef burglar.

What do you call a failed lion tamer?

Claude Bottom.

What do you call an unlucky cat?

A catastrophe.

PUT THAT DOG DOWN!

A man takes his Golden Retriever to the vet.

"My dog's cross-eyed. Is there anything you can do for him?"

"Well," says the vet. "Let's take a look at him."

So he picks the dog up and examines his eyes, then checks his teeth and ears.

Finally, the vet says, "I'm afraid I'm going to have to put the dog down."

"Oh no, Doctor! You're going to put him down because he's cross-eyed?"

"No, because he's really heavy."

What do you call a sheep that says "Quack"?

Bilingual.

What do you call a woman crossing a river?

Bridget.

What do you call a camel with no humps?

A horse.

What do you call a small mother?

Minimum.

How do you stop your dog barking in the front of the car?

Put it in the back.

What do you get if you cross a bridge with a car?

To the other side of the river.

What do you call a cat with no legs?

Anything you like — she won't be able to come anyway.

What do you get if you cross a kangaroo with a sweater?

A woolly jumper.

What do you get if you cross a car park with a safari park?

Double yellow lions.

What do you call a man floating on a raft?

Bob.

Mother: What did you learn at school today?

Kid: Not enough, I have to go back tomorrow.

MONSTER
LAUGHS

HOW MUCH IS THAT BRAIN IN THE WINDOW?

An alien walks into a shop. He tells the shop owner that he has come from all the way from Mars and wants to buy a brain for research. Pointing to a brain, the alien asks, "How much is this one?"

"Well, that one is a monkey's brain and it's £20," the owner explains.

"Ok, how much is that one?" the alien asks.

"Well, that one is a kid's brain and it's £100," the owner explains.

"And how much is that one?" the alien asks.

"That one is a teacher's brain and it is £500," the owner explains.

"Why so expensive?" the alien asks.

"Well, it has hardly ever been used!"

DOCTOR, DOCTOR

Did you hear about the monster who was mad about snooker? He went to the doctor because he didn't feel well.

"What do you eat?" asked the doctor.

"For breakfast I have a couple of red snooker balls, and at lunchtime I have a black, a yellow and two pinks. I have a brown one as a snack in the afternoon, and then a blue and another pink for dinner."

"I know why you don't feel well," exclaimed the doctor. "You're not getting enough greens."

MONSTER BURP!

One day a man went to his doctor claiming that he had swallowed a monster. Nothing his doctor said would make him change his mind.

Finally the doctor gave him an anaesthetic and put him into a deep sleep. When the man woke up, the doctor was standing beside his bed. In the doctor's hands was a great big green monster.

"Nothing more to worry about," said the doctor. "We operated on you and took this monster out."

"Who are you trying to kid?" asked the man. "The monster I swallowed was a blue one."

IN LOVING MEMORY

A boy was walking behind a
hearse with a big monster on
a lead. Behind them stretched
a long line of mourners.
"What happened?" asked a boy
who was passing by.
"The monster bit my sister, and
she died of fright."
"Can I borrow it?" the passer-
by asked.
The boy pointed behind him.
"Get in the queue," he said.

ART ATTACK

A very snooty man was
walking around an art gallery.
He stopped by one particular
painting and called over the
gallery assistant.
"I suppose this picture of a
hideous monster is what you
call modern art," he said very
pompously.
"No, sir," replied the assistant,
"That's what we call a mirror."

BIG HEAD!

This young monster came home from school one day, crying his eyes out.

"What's the matter, darling?" asked his mother.

"It's all the other children at school," he wept. "They keep teasing me and saying that I've got a big head."

"Of course you haven't got a big head," said Mrs Monster. "Just ignore them. Now, will you do a little bit of shopping for me? I need a sack of potatoes, ten cartons of milk, twenty loaves of bread, eight cans of baked beans and a water melon."

"All right," said the little monster. "Can I take your shopping bag?"

"Oh, that's broken, I'm afraid," said Mrs Monster. "But it doesn't matter — just put the things in your hat."

YOU MUST BE CHOKING

A man went into a café with a big, vicious monster on a lead.
"Sorry, Sir," said the owner. "But that creature looks dangerous. You'll have to tie him up outside."
So the man took the monster outside, and came back and ordered a coffee.
He was just finishing it when a lady came in and said, "Whose monster is that outside?"
'Mine," said the man, beaming with pride.
" Well, I'm sorry," the lady replied. "But my dog's just killed him."
"Killed him! What kind of dog do you have?"
"A miniature poodle," said the lady.
"But how could a miniature poodle kill my great big monster?"
"She got stuck in his throat and choked him."

POLICE ORDERS

A policeman stopped a man who was walking along with a monster and ordered him to take it to the zoo at once.

The next day the policeman saw the same man, still with the monster.

"I thought I told you to take that monster to the zoo," he said.

"I did," said the man. "And now I'm taking him to the pictures."

BROTHERLY LOVE

Kelly: Yesterday I took my brother to see "The Monster From The Swamp" at the cinema.

Susie: What was he like?

Kelly: Oh, about ten feet tall, with a horrible, slimy head, and a bolt through his neck.

Susie: I don't mean your brother, silly — what was the monster like?

KING OF THE JUNGLE

A gorilla was walking through the jungle when he came across a deer in a clearing. The gorilla roared, "Who is the king of the jungle?"

The deer replied, "Oh, you are, sir."

The gorilla walked off pleased with himself. Soon he met a zebra drinking at a water hole. "Who is the king of the jungle?" he roared.

"Oh, you are, sir," replied the zebra.

The gorilla walked off pleased. Then he came across an elephant. "Who is the king of the jungle?" he roared.

Suddenly, the elephant picked up the gorilla and threw him on the ground and jumped on him.

The gorilla dragged himself up out of the dirt and said, "Okay, okay, there's no need to get mad just because you don't know the answer."

BRAVEHEART

Bill: Did I ever tell you about the time I came face to face with a very fierce gorilla?

Joe: No, what happened?

Bill: Well, I stood there, without a gun. The gorilla looked at me and snarled and roared and beat his chest. Then it came closer and closer...

Joe: What did you do?

Bill: Oh, I'd had enough, so I moved on to the next cage.

GOOD LITTLE MONSTER

Did you hear about the very well-behaved little monster? When he was good, his father would give him 10p and a pat on the head.
By the time he was 16 years old he had £100 in the bank and his head was totally flat.

BAD MANNERS

Three monsters called Manners,
Mind-Your-Own-Business and
Trouble were on holiday
together. One day, Trouble
went missing. Manners and
Mind-Your-Own-Business
decided to report to the police
that Trouble was missing.
When they got to the police
station, Manners got frightened
and decided to stay outside.
Mind-You-Own-Business went in
to report the loss. The police
officer asked him his name, to
which the monster replied,
"Mind-Your-Own-Business."
The desk sergeant crossly said,
"Where's your manners?"
Mind-Your-Own-Business
replied, "Outside."
On hearing such rudeness, the
desk sergeant said, "Are you
looking for Trouble?"
to which Mind-Your-Own-
Business quickly replied,
"Yes, please!"

WHO'S AN UGLY BABY?

One day a station porter found a woman with a baby in her arms sitting in the waiting room. She was sobbing miserably. The porter went up to her and asked what was wrong.

"Some people were in the waiting room just now and they were very rude about my little boy," she cried. "They said that he was horribly ugly."

"There, there, please don't cry," said the porter, kindly. "I'll get you a nice cup of tea to cheer you up."

"Thank you, that would be lovely," replied the woman, wiping her eyes. "You're a very kind man."

"That's all right. Don't mention it," said the porter. "While I'm at it, would you like a banana for your little gorilla?"

OVER TO YOU

New jokes are being created all
the time. So we are constantly
adding to our files to make sure
we have all the best jokes
around. If you or your friends
hear any jokes that you really
like, let us know about them.
You can e-mail us at:
jokes@michaelomarabooks.com

We'll let you know if
your jokes are going
to be included
in the next book.

Thanks.